# ON COMMON GROUND

# ON COMMON GROUND

*Photographs from the Crossroads of the New South*

BY CHIP SIMONE

*Foreword by Andrew Young*

MERCER UNIVERSITY PRESS

MACON, GEORGIA

1996

ISBN 0-86554-486-7

# On Common Ground

Photographs from the Crossroads of the New South
by Chip Simone

On Common Ground copyright © 1996 Mercer University Press
Photographs © 1996 Chip Simone

The paper used in this publication meets the minimum requirements of American National Standards for Information Sciences—Permanence of Paper for printed Library Materials, ANSI Z39.48-1984.

Library of Congress Cataloging-in-Publication Data on file at the Library of Congress

*For my wife Katya*

A carnival circles the

park endlessly, on foot, bike, in-line skates, drugs; electrons

spinning around some protean nucleus. Muscle men, sex kittens, athletes,

fools. Snake men, dog handlers, ferret lovers. God's children, dressed in

Joseph's multi-colored robes. "Look at me!" *the tattoos, nose rings,*

*and shaved heads shout.* "Love me," *they whisper.*

—VINCENT COPPOLA, *ATLANTA MAGAZINE*, NOVEMBER, 1994

# FOREWORD

THE DRAMATIC CHANGES THAT HAVE TAKEN PLACE IN the American South over the past forty years did not come about by accident. These changes evolved through the actions of many people who responded to the violence and hatred that surrounded them with great courage and magnificent faith.

By God's amazing grace I have been a part of one of our nation's most powerful periods of history. Not even in my wildest dreams, could I have anticipated the remarkable outcome of our struggle for justice and equality. I have been a witness to the triumph of the human spirit.

Little did I know that a series of simple decisions would intertwine my personal destiny with that of the modern South and the lives of two great Southern visionaries—Martin Luther King Jr. and President Jimmy Carter. Working with these two men of great faith and leadership enabled me to see the struggle for human dignity as a universal struggle. Indeed, the American South was at the forefront of this effort. The South was being transformed and that transformation, in turn, reshaped the world.

I came back to the South after the Hartford Seminary to serve two small communities where no one else was likely to go. In Thomasville and Beachton, Georgia, I began my lessons in discernment, lessons learned from elderly citizens who taught me to see each human being as unique. Considering that this was the Deep South of the 1950s, this was a powerful message.

In the eyes of the world, many Southern cities have become icons for the region—Memphis and Nashville for popular music, New Orleans for Jazz and the finest cuisine on God's green earth. Birmingham, Montgomery, and Selma, sites of some of the most difficult days of the civil rights struggle, remain etched in our collective memories as emblems of the price of freedom.

I am proud to say that Atlanta has come to symbolize the idea of the New South—the progressive South that so many of us have struggled to achieve. The beautiful Atlanta skyline of today is clear evidence that Atlanta's economic strength is a powerful engine that pulls forward the entire region. We count among our corporate citizens some of the giants of modern industry and some of our country's brightest and most innovative entrepreneurs. We see in our neighborhoods some of the most desirable places to live in the nation.

Atlanta began at the intersection of two railroad tracks in a virgin forest. Less than 166 years later this modern city has become a crossroad of the world. When the Centennial Olympic games are held here in 1996, we will be one of the world's busiest and most visible. Who could have imagined how far we would come? Of course there are many different Atlantas in my mind. It isn't the same city I found when I first came here. It has gone through some remarkable changes and led the region in a progressive direction. I have even played a part in some of those changes, first as a congressman and then as mayor of Atlanta for two terms.

Chip Simone sees the city of Atlanta in much the same way as I do. There is a feeling in his photographs that evokes the essential core of Atlanta today. Atlanta has always been at the crossroads of the New South, and as the cradle of America's civil rights movement it has become an important part of our nation's moral ground. Chip's striking images show us that Atlanta's playful center, Piedmont Park, serves as an important model as our public common. What has made Atlanta unique among Southern cities is our search for balance and commonality and our efforts to solve problems after consideration and participation from all levels and classes of our society. We continue to work at this and while we aren't a perfect community, we have come a great distance. These efforts have enabled us to progress culturally and economically, to attract an increasingly diverse population, and to produce significant social changes that are admired throughout the world. Chip's photographs capture the spirit of those changes and reveal our increasing diversity.

On the way to a peaceful and prosperous world we continue to face the great challenge of finding among people from different cultures, backgrounds, lifestyles, and points of view: that shared quality which unites us into our common humanity.

In these photographs from Piedmont Park, from the emotional heart of our city, the heart of the New South, Chip has expressed with a beautiful honesty that humanity which is our Common Ground.

*—Andrew Young,*
*New York,*
*October 1995*

# INTRODUCTION: ON COMMON GROUND

THE AMERICAN SOUTH HAS UNDERGONE A remarkable transformation over the last forty years, yet the images associated with the region remain trapped in the past. The South's obsession with its own history and the romantic icons made popular by myth and fiction have enabled the stereotype and the cliché to become the dominant perception of Southern life. But the crucible of the civil rights era, coupled with the economic success of cities like Atlanta, has created a new Southern reality, one that calls for a new set of images.

When I moved from New York City to Atlanta in 1972, I looked forward to becoming a part of something new. In those heady days, Atlanta was young and full of itself. Caught in a time-warp between the sins of its Jim Crow past and the lure of a limitless future, the capitol city of the American South was struggling to redefine its identity. Despite the explosive urbanization of the region, however, much art in the South remained rooted in rural lore and the historic past: Charleston, Savannah, the Low Country, the hard and unforgiving land and, of course, Scarlet and Tara. Like all good acolytes I made the pilgrimages and visited the shrines, but, no matter how hard I looked in those places, I rarely found in any of them a reflection of myself.

I have always been a street photographer. I prefer the unpredictable nature of the city as the source of my images. I was raised in the inner city and to this day I am seduced by the visual drama of its fractured light, shifting energy, and the complex and diverse mix of eccentric characters that only a street culture can grow. Specifically I am from "Shrewsbury Street," the Italian-American neighborhood of Worcester, Massachusetts, that takes its name from the main drag that serves as its spine and connects the downtown with the village of Shrewsbury just east across Lake Quinsigamond. As is the case with most working-class tenement ghettos, social life in our community clustered outside of the home on the corners under streetlights, in doorways, and drive-in restaurants, and, of course, the sanctum sanctorum, the all-night diner. While growing up I would eavesdrop on Italian immigrants congregated in Cristoforo Columbus Park to play "Bocci," gossip, avoid gainful employment, and make fun of Americans. My grandfather Bartolomeo was a noted storyteller and came to be known as the "Mayor" of Shrewsbury Street. I received my first camera as a Christmas gift from my parents in 1956 and twenty-six years later conducted a major photographic study of Shrewsbury Street with funds from the National Endowment for the

Arts. The photographs are now in the permanent collection of the Worcester Historical Museum. I wanted to continue the family story-telling tradition using pictures rather than words. The night that the exhibit opened, so did the heavens. Despite the downpour, more than four hundred people came, passing under the twenty-by-forty-foot Italian flag, setting a new attendance record for the museum. They came from the "neighborhood." Most had never been to the historical museum before. Some baked cookies and pizzas, as if for an Italian wedding. It brought tears to my eyes. These good people, the subjects of my photographs, were eager to look into the mirror and see themselves and to see how they would be portrayed to future generations.

I grew up surrounded by a complex and diverse community; truck drivers and laborers, grocers and short-order cooks, priests and bookies, loan-sharks and thieves. They had colorful nicknames like "Teddy Rags," "Nicky Sho-Sho," "Crevice," "The Hub," "Joe Magic Hair." There was even a guy named "Killer" who my father claimed got his name the old fashioned way. This was street life in the panoramic sense. It was rich and eccentric and dangerous. It was intricately drawn and as complex as a story by Damon Runyon. There was cruelty and compassion, generosity and greed, violence and romance all on one street. Most importantly this was the inspiration for my vision, my view of life. To this day, it is the life on the street that draws me to the street. It is among these endless individuals—flawed and fascinating and glowingly human—that I find the clearest reflection of myself.

Today most Southerners live in population centers. The South is the fastest growing part of America attracting new residents from anywhere and everywhere else. The mint julep of the genteel past is being replaced by a spicy cocktail of racial harmonics, cultural diversity, and alternative lifestyles with a twist of raw ambition. No place reflects these changes more than Piedmont Park, the century-old green space in the heart of Atlanta's midtown that was racially segregated until 1962. Today the park serves as the public common for the entire city: black and white, rich and poor, straight and gay. The park is a fertile environment where new Southern life can be found in all of its forms, defining in the process what we have become as a community.

My photographs of Piedmont Park challenge the traditional view of the region and offer a fresh look at life in today's South. These images are not meant to be documentary or definitive, but instead, evidence of a deeply personal odyssey.

I went to the park twice a day, every day for a year, with my camera and a simple agenda: to remain curious and non-judgmental; to look closer and deeper than the day before; to make strong and compelling photographs. Each morning and afternoon, when the light was best, I walked the park with my dog Paris, an eighty-five-pound pure white German Shepherd. As gentle as she is beautiful, Paris turned strangers into friends and helped create a warm and trusting atmosphere for me to work in. Her presence was critical to my being able to produce intimate images of people that I had met only moments earlier. I could not have produced this body of work without her at my side.

I never knew what I might see at Piedmont park. Some days it seemed that I was the only one in the park. At other times I had to be careful not to be run over by a roller-blader, skate-boarder, jogger, or biker. The mood of the park was never constant; it changed with the weather, the seasons, the time of day and the day of the week.

As a picture maker I found the most compelling images not at the center of this protean social whirl but at its edges. The offbeat, eccentric non-conformists yielded the strongest pictures. But, without question, this public place, this common ground, attracts the richest, most diverse, most representative cross section of life in the modern, urban South. While it might not sit well with those invested in perpetuating the mythology of the "moonbeam and magnolia" South or the "barefoot and pregnant" redneck South, this is today's South. The resulting images in this book represent the visceral and emotional responses to spontaneous encounters and unexpected observations. These photographs are individual pieces of a rich, intricate mosaic of life in the modern South free of cliché, prejudice, and sentimentality.

When taken as a whole, this unconventional collection of photographs is intended to go beyond the descriptive to become symbolic of a new Southern spirit: confident, relaxed, and modern. Like a mosaic, *On Common Ground* is the sum of the pieces that tells the whole story, pieces somehow connected because I have seen them.

*Chip Simone*
*Atlanta*
*July, 1995*

# ON COMMON GROUND

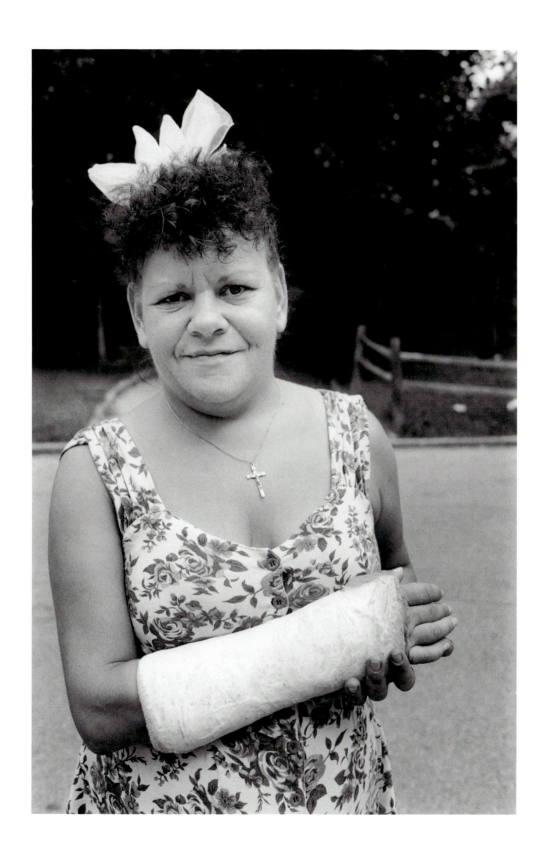

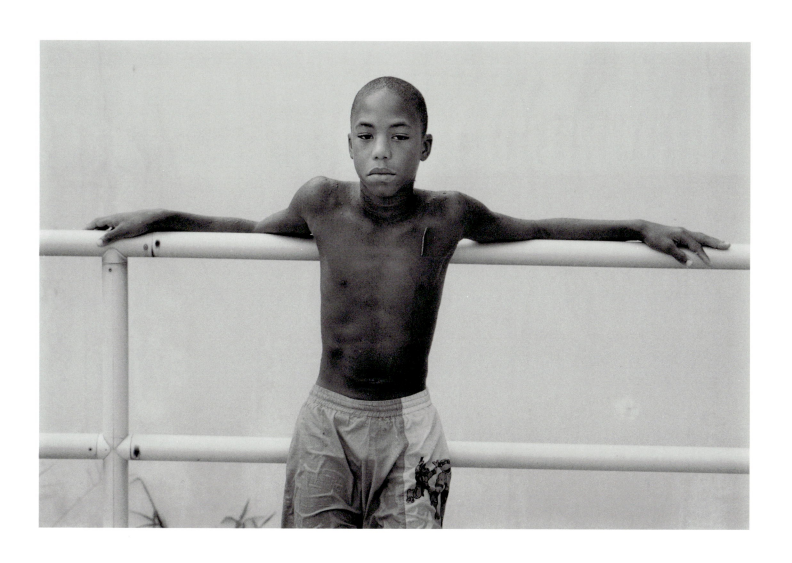

80

# In Gratitude

*The photographer and publisher gratefully acknowledge the many contributors whose financial support made this book possible.*

*The great generosity at the very start of this journey of three special donors established a foundation of support and paved the way for all other contributors:*
Ray and Mary Grace Miller
*of Atlanta, and to*
Father James Michael Doyle
*of Souix Falls, South Dakota.*

*For their substantial contributions to this project:*

Charles S. Ackerman

Dr. Walter Ray Davis Jr.

Harold and Betsy Hansen

Jennings and Jill Hertz

Dr. Joe and Adair Massey

Jim and Lynn Myer Rollins

Dr. Paul Sternberg

Ruth T. West

*We are also grateful to these many generous individuals:*

David and Betsy Baker

John and Beverly Baker

Temmi Barkin-Leeds

Dr. and Mrs. Stephen Barnett

Milton and Paula Lawton Bevington

Dr. Dorothy E. Brawley

Dr. and Mrs. R. L. Bunnen

Harry and Eleanor Callahan

Larry Doyle

Jerry Farber

Richard and Sharan Flexner

Sidney and Roni Funk

Melita Easters Hayes

Susan A. Hancock and Harry L. Miller

Laura Heery

Tom Houck

Clay and Jane Jackson

Edwina Johnson

Seth Kirschenbaum

Nicholas Lotito

Maruice and Gloria Maloof

Allen and Sara McDaniel

Barbara Pyle

Louis Regenstein

Claude T. Sullivan

Judy Tabb

Steve Walsh and Angela Dorries

# ACKNOWLEDGMENTS

In April 1994, four months after I began making the photographs that appear in this book, my father Jack Simone died following a long illness. Jack was a social creature who took great delight in observing human behavior, especially the candid, revealing gesture. As a young boy I learned that if you look at people a certain way you will see things that others don't see. Learning to see the wonder of ordinary life was my father's greatest gift to me. I regret deeply that he did not live to see this book published.

The photographs in this book were made possible through the generous cooperation of the hundreds of Atlantans that I met in Piedmont Park. Their good nature and easy, spontaneous trust is a testament to the spirit of the New South.

Designer David Laufer was my guardian angel throughout this project. He guided me, with patience and humor, through the minefield of book production and protected the high standards and values that mattered to me most.

Art patron Ruth West suggested that I bring my work to Mercer University Press. I did and this book happened.

To Mercer University Press, Scott Nash, and especially my editor Jon Peede, a young man wise beyond his years.

A project such as this is a big burden for a small press. It took courage and conviction. I thank them for both.

The photographer Joel Meyerowitz suggested that I contact Alan Blazar at Blazing Graphics about printing this book. Look through these pages and you'll see why. It's a dream come true. Bless them both.

To the many individuals who were so generous in support of this project in both material and spiritual ways: my best friend in Atlanta Jerry Farber who always believed in me; Melita Easters Hayes who has supported my work generously; Ray Miller and Fr. Jim Doyle who gave the first big push to make this book a reality; photographer Steven DiRado my friend and colleague; Andrew Young and Doug Gatlin who honored me by becoming associated with this book; Wendy Rhein who helped make me look professional; Charles Ackerman who was generous with both resources and wisdom; Lucinda Bunnen who opened her home and invited support; Vince Coppola for his gift of words; High Museum curator Ellen Dugan, her assistant Anna Bloomfield, Jerry Prine, Jane Jackson, and Angela Dorries for their faith and encouragement. The guys in the weight room at the Decatur-Dekalb YMCA whose good natured ribbing kept me grounded in the real world. Thank you all.

To Earl T. Edwards who was homeless and living in the park during the early months of this project. Earl shared with me his insights about life in the park, kept me company and protected me. He now has a job and a home and I'm proud to be his friend.

To Piedmont Park itself for being so tolerant and available to all of Atlanta. Piedmont Park is one of this city's greatest assets and deserves more attention and better care than it has received in recent years. There is a real need to protect the park from overuse and to restore the health of this living thing, this common ground.

I hope that this book helps to raise Atlantan's awareness of the tremendous value Piedmont park holds for them.

I would like to add a special note of appreciation to photographer Harry Callahan, who now lives in Atlanta, for continuing to inspire me through his lifelong and continuing dedication to his work.

I would also like to acknowledge my mother Louise Simone and my sister Elaine Simone for accepting my love for photography from the very beginning.

And finally I wish to thank my wife Kathy Egan. It has been my great good fortune to share life with a woman of such beauty and ability. I dedicate this book in her honor.

# TECHNICAL NOTES

"You cannot receive the smiles and blushes of your lover through your attorney, no matter how diligent he may be." –*Rabindranath Tagore*
*Nobel Prize winning poet, on the art of translating poetry*

*On Common Ground* is the product of two extraordinary efforts. The first effort is that of an individual poet creating images. The second effort is that of the team that translated the smiles, blushes, and other subtleties in these pictures into a book that remains remarkably true–technically and emotionally–to the originals. While Chip's photographs might have been possible a few years ago, a book version of them at this level of quality would not.

Virtually every new innovation in printing that could be applied to the creation of excellent black and white reproductions was at least considered, in many cases tried and retried, before the final formula was settled. The outcome is, we feel, a landmark first use of these technologies together. A synopsis follows.

The printing press cannot reproduce shades of gray. Each point on the printing plate can only deliver all ink or no ink. The printing industry has expended a great deal of ingenuity attempting to capture and control the luxurious tones of black and white photographs in print. It does this by breaking those continuous tone prints into groups of small dots; virtually every school child with a magnifying glass has examined the coarse dot pattern in a newspaper photo. For a long time high-quality reproduction meant ever smaller dot patterns. First 200-line, then 400-line, even in a few cases 1200-line halftones appeared. Because these dots were infinitely variable in both size and shape, they yielded high detail, beautiful tonal scales, but also required extreme skill and cost to create the dots and print them. Often the extra detail and tonal range offered by fine line screens was lost or distorted because of dot gain. Dot gain, the tendency of small dots to pick up more ink than their size would suggest, made some areas of the photo appear to darken or "gain."

The printing press also cannot match, in a single impression, the rich tonal range of a quality black and white print. Duotone and tritone reproduction–the practice of printing the same image in multiple impressions–reached a fairly high level of refinement even before the digital revolution hit printing. Dot gain and loss were again limiting factors. *On Common Ground*'s tritones use three different images of the photograph, each printed from a separate cylinder of the printing press, each responsible for a different section of the tonal scale. This allows for both the added depth needed, and the control on press to adjust the printed sheet to match the original.

Blazing Graphics ran several tests to achieve the smoothest tonalities. The images in this book were screened stochastically, meaning that they use a small, randomized dot pattern on all plates. This further enhances the textural qualities of the subjects (see illustration.)

Since the invention of offset lithography, balancing the ink and water levels on the press has been the limiting factor in many attempts at high-quality reproduction. Recently, the development of waterless offset has moved from curiosity to cutting edge. The decision to print this book waterless made it possible to keep bright, clean highlights, and rich dense shadows, and hold maximum detail at every point in the tonal scale in between. Eliminating water allows the printing of a sharp, clean dot, which will not gain or lose in size, and the stochastic screening gave us the ability to render Chip's images into extremely small, yet precisely controlled dots.

Another decision which added synergy was the ink. Soy-based inks have been available for conventional offset for a decade or more, and have gained popularity because, being organically based, they are environmentally friendly. Recently Toyo of Japan began formulating the vegetable based inks for waterless printing. In

conventional halftone
(one plate, magnified
10x)

Stochastic halftone
(one plate, magnified
10x)

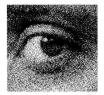
Stochastic tritone
(all three plates,
magnified 10x)

addition to the environmental advantage, soy inks fit well with this book because they offer a dense, rich black, somewhat akin to the legendary look of sheetfed gravure, a look very congruent with the feel of the original prints and the emotional content of the subjects.

Our ability to create tritone separations which could take advantage of this convergence of technical advances was enhanced by the ability to preview the separations quickly on an Iris printer. The Iris is essentially a very large and precise color ink jet printer. Once a scan looked right on the computer, we could go quickly to Iris. Once the Iris looked right, we could go on to the expense of stochastic screening, and later press proofing, with a minimum of waste. All of this is a very recent way of working; and the proof positive of these many new ideas may make *On Common Ground* a harbinger of new levels of excellence in photographic books.

The team at Blazing Graphics responsible for developing and realizing this coalition of techniques deserves great credit for their professionalism and insight: In the prepress area, Ray Gagne as foreman, with Chris Colbert and Elliott Lewin. The Pressroom foreman was Nunzio "Togo" Pallazo, the lead pressman Mike Harrop. Barry Walsh planned the production, Maureen White handled traffic, and Rick Trahan was the Production Supervisor. Alan Blazar's enthusiasm and zeal for quality made my efforts as designer rewarding and pleasurable.     *—David Laufer*

# Colophon

The photographs in *On Common Ground* were made using Nikon F4 cameras and Nikkor lenses. The images were recorded on Kodak's T-Max 100 film. The negatives were printed on Oriental VC Plus enlarging paper through an Apo Rodagon enlarging lens.

The text type is Bitstream's Arrus, composed in Quark Xpress on a MacIntosh Quadra 840 AV, and output to a Linotronic 300.

The paper is 100 lb. Allegro Silk Text, manufactured in Switzerland and supplied by WWF Paper.

The photographs were scanned on a  DS 608 Laser Scanner, Graphics, and output as stochastic tritones on a Agfa Avantra 44 'Bigfoot' Imagesetter. The text was printed by offset lithography on a 26"x 40" Mitsubishi 3F six color waterless press, by Blazing Graphics, Cranston, Rhode Island.

The book was bound by Zonne Bookbinders, Inc., Chicago, Illinois, in Arrestrox C cloth, made by Holliston Mills.

Mercer University Press, Macon, Georgia 31210.
ISBN 0-86554-486-7
MUP/H381

Book design by David Laufer, Roswell, Georgia.